Unlo[cking]
of Children's Dreams

Stacey Linsalata

Special thanks to my dear friends, Emily and Noah Baer and Jinny Gerber, for editing this book for me and trying to make sense of all my random thoughts!

Unlocking the Mystery of Children's Dreams
Copyright © 2016 Stacey Linsalata
Published by Dream Culture
www.cultureofdreaming.com
Email: hilltop568@hotmail.com

Cover photo © canstockphotos.com
All other photos and clipart © canstockphotos.com

Resources used were the Holy Bible and The Psalms-Poetry on Fire (The Passion Translation)

No part of this book in any form (electronic, mechanical, photocopying or recording) may be reproduced unless written consent is given in advance by the author. Permission is granted for the duplication of these materials for the purpose of sharing with multiple leaders within the same church or organization.

Table of Contents

Forward..V

Preface..VII

1. Created to Dream...1

2. But Why Dreams?..9

3. Imagine That!...19

4. Vivid Visions..29

5. Reasons for Nightmares................................35

6. Warriors in Training......................................45

7. Finding the Source..55

8. Discovering Dream Language.....................65

9. The Language of the Spirit..........................73

10. Creating a Culture of Dreaming.................81

11. Mystery Solved...or is it?............................89

Endnotes...97

Forward

Stacey has inspired me to unlock the mysteries of my dreams and the dreams of my children! She has unpacked the many layered aspects of dreaming from the natural to the supernatural and has redefined how parents should look at and approach children's dreams.

Although dreaming is a very natural thing we have all done at one time or another, it also can be the most supernatural way God speaks to us if we are willing to listen. Stacey uses personal experiences, the word of God, humor, and creative family activities to draw the reader into an exciting, line by line, approach to unlocking the mysteries of dreams not only for children but the entire family. The world of dreaming has been opened up to me and now I have the tools needed to teach my children about it too.

-Alicia White, director and founder of Chosen Stones Family Ministry and Ohio direction for Kids in Ministry International

Preface

Mysterious, comical, scary, perplexing, imaginative, insightful … am I talking about dreams or children? The answer is: both! Dreams can be all those things, and so can children. When you put them both together, you have a combination that can make a grown man (or woman) cry!

Dreams seem complicated enough on their own—let alone throwing in a child's wild imagination and endless supply of energy! But dreams don't have to be quite so perplexing. God has given us keys to help unlock the mystery of not only our kids' dreams, but our own dreams as well.

I don't claim to have discovered all the keys to understanding dreams. I believe there are so many that there will always be more to find. I'm only on a journey to uncover as many keys as I can. In this book I want to share with you some of the keys that I have found over the last few years that I hope will give you insights into this mysterious world. Before I start sharing these keys with you, I want to briefly tell you where my journey to discovery began.

About 15 years ago a friend introduced me to the idea that dreams had meaning to them. Even though I had been a dreamer my whole life, it never occurred to me that there could be messages from God hidden within my dreams. That one simple notion started a series of events that I can only describe as a domino effect that began to happen in my life.

This same friend introduced me to John Paul Jackson's materials from Streams Ministries International. The hunger to discover the hidden meaning of dreams was so stirred in my spirit that I began to devour whatever materials I could get my hands on. At the same time, I began to experience a lot of unusual events during the nighttime. I knew they weren't all dreams, and it compelled me to dig in even deeper.

During my quest to understand more about dreams, I was introduced to a man who had recently graduated from John Paul Jackson's school of ministry. He was now living in my area and teaching classes about dreams. My husband and I immediately became connected with him and he mentored us for several years. During that time, I was discovering more and more keys to understanding dreams. I began to really seek God for the gift of not only dream interpretation but also mysteries, riddles, and deep sayings of God.

As the gift of interpretation was growing inside me, I started a Facebook group called "Culture of Dreaming." It was going to be a place where I could share with others what I had been learning. Members of the group could also post dreams to be interpreted. The group is still there to this day. People are not only able to post dreams, but also able to practice interpreting other people's dreams as well.

I also had a desire to teach my children everything I was learning about dreams. I looked for materials that I could use to teach them, but I couldn't find anything for kids. I was also leading the children's ministry at my local church. I felt God laid it on my heart to teach a dream workshop to the children there. I knew if I were going to teach them, I would have to write my own materials. My goal was to take the depth of what John Paul Jackson and others had taught me and break it down into its simplest form, so that even a child could understand it.

As I was preparing to teach the workshop, I received a download from the Holy Spirit of creative ideas to make dreaming fun for kids. I started sharing these ideas with others, including Becky Fischer of Kids in Ministry International. She loved the ideas and encouraged me to start writing a curriculum for Sunday school teachers. That is how "Encounters in the Night" was born. "Encounters in the Night" is a 12 lesson curriculum that teaches kids the foundation of dreams, visions, and imaginations. It's written specifically for a classroom.

As I started writing "Encounters in the Night," new revelations and new keys to understanding dreams were being given to me. I was not only relying on what I had been taught by others; I was now being taught directly by the Holy Spirit. Writing that curriculum is what launched me into developing a ministry called Culture of Dreaming. Culture of Dreaming is not simply for kids but also for the entire family. My passion is to develop a family culture that values dreams and the messages within them.

After writing the curriculum, I started teaching dream workshops to both kids and adults. In 2016 I had the privilege of recording a dream session for the School of Supernatural Children's Ministry in North Dakota, teaching kids about dreams in Boston at a One Ten/Lou Engel conference, and doing dream interpretations on the streets of Iquitos, Peru.

In my traveling, I discovered there was a need for resources to help parents teach their children about dreams. The curriculum was great for teaching in a classroom setting, but I needed to write a book that would be a useful tool for the home. And here we have it—"Unlocking the Mystery of Children's Dreams!"

So, as you can see, once the first domino was knocked down, it hit another, which hit another, which is still in a chain reaction to this day. I look forward with great excitement to see what new and creative ideas God will give me for teaching kids about dreams. God and His dreams are truly my passion, and I hope this passion for dreams will start a domino effect in your life and your children's lives as well!

Chapter 1
Created to Dream

In order for parents to truly begin to understand their children's dreams, it only seems appropriate to start at the very beginning. You might think I mean the beginning of this book but in fact, I'm talking about the beginning of creation itself!

If you can grasp God's amazing design for your children as dreamers, you'll begin to feel an excitement each night they lie down as you wait for something supernatural to unfold. And no, I'm not just talking about the excitement you feel when the kids are finally asleep, although, that DOES deserves a certain level of excitement!

But a new level of excitement will begin to build as you think about all the grand revelations and new adventures that await your children as they have encounters with the living God through dreams and visions of the night. All of a sudden you'll find yourself bursting into their rooms each morning asking about all the dreams they had that night. Of course, if you're not a morning person, it would be more than acceptable to hold off your excitement until breakfast ... and several cups of coffee.

So to start our journey, I want to take you all the way back to Genesis and combine that with what science is discovering about the origins of dreaming. From here we can build a picture of God's amazing design for our bodies and dreaming.

The first chapter of Genesis is the account of creation, including the creation of man and woman. God already had everything figured out before He started the creation process. He knew exactly what we would need to live and thrive on this earth. He built within our DNA everything we would need to not only thrive on this earth, but also communicate with Him. He was not about to create us out of divine love and then leave us with no way of communicating with Him, no way to receive instruction and guidance.

Of course the most ideal form of communication is what we see in the garden: those one-on-one chats Adam and Eve had with God. However, it was clear from the beginning that God intended to also communicate with us through other means. When Adam and Even sinned, I don't believe our brain structure changed. What I mean is, our brains are still wired the same way they were at creation, because it's simply our original design. The blueprints didn't change because of sin. The blueprints show that we were designed to dream from the very beginning.

Have you ever thought about the fact that you never had to tell yourself to start dreaming when you were a baby? It's just a natural part of who you've always been. God designed your body in a way that you rarely have to think about how it's functioning. You just know it is! You aren't stopping to tell your heart how to beat or your brain how to think ... well, OK — maybe you do have to do that last one on occasion!

The point is, we don't question why we were given our brains or any other vital organs — we just know we need them! And yet, I hear so many people question the necessity for dreams because they don't recognize that it's an integral part of their design.

The only reason we have the ability to dream is because God put it within our DNA to be a dreamer. It's just as much a vital part of our design as lungs are for breathing, eyes are for seeing, or ears are for hearing.

Somehow we've gotten our priorities out of line and we've elevated our physical attributes above our spiritual ones. I think it's time for a shift in our thinking! It's time to rediscover the hidden parts of our design—the ancient forms of communication called dreams, visions, and imaginations.

That's right … I said imagination! The imagination isn't just something reserved for small children and then we slowly outgrow it; at least that's not the way it's supposed to be! I'll talk more about the role of the imagination as it relates to dreams in chapter three.

Now that we've gone back to the original blueprints of our design, let's look at the science of dreaming and see if it supports God's original plan for us as dreamers. As you might be able to guess, the science behind dreaming lines up pretty well with God's original design and that's exactly why I'm getting ready to tell you about it!

There was a fascinating study done by a scientific research group in the 1970's. [a] They discovered that fetuses almost exclusively spend their *entire* time in the womb in a state of R.E.M.

R.E.M. stands for rapid eye movement and it's the stage where we dream. As adults we move in and out of dream cycles throughout the entire night. One medical website states adults spend about 20% of their night in a state of dreaming. [b] Now compare that to what the research is showing about fetuses spending almost their entire time in a state of dreaming. During our most vital stages of development, which will shape who we become, God designed us so that we spend nearly that entire time of development in a state of constant dreaming. It's that amazing!

When I read these findings I began to wonder what a fetus could possibly be dreaming about. The research group offered the suggestion that they would be dreaming about lights and sounds they were experiencing. I began to really meditate on this and I felt God placed something into my spirit. I believe God is using this most foundational time in our developing lives to download dreams to us about what He created us to be. He's using this time to seal His destiny into us.

Now obviously we can't remember the dreams we had in the womb! I believe as we grow and begin to come into our destiny of who God created us to be that we somehow get glimpses of what those dreams were. If this is true, it certainly should change the way we perceive our children's dreams! No longer can we view our children's dreams as nothing more than an overactive imagination, but instead we start looking for hidden messages of divine destiny and purpose.

Now let's get back to the facts! The research goes on to say that including the time in the womb and the first two weeks of our lives, we have already had more dreams then we will the rest of our lives combined! Newborn babies can instantly enter into a state of dreaming without going through sleep cycles like most adults do. Considering how much time a newborn spends sleeping, we can only imagine how many dreams they must be having those first couple of months! One article said infants spend at least 50% of their time in a state of dreaming. [c]

Think about it ... do you remember feeding your newborn as they were drifting off to sleep and noticed their eyes were moving back and forth under their heavy eyelids? That's R.E.M. Your newborn was already in a state of dreaming while they were still drinking. That baby didn't have to tell itself to dream any more than it had to tell its heart to beat. Why? Because dreaming is the Creator's design for us!

> **When we truly understand that dreaming is part of God's design for us, and that He stamped it into our development and birth, how could we *not* place a very high value on the gift of dreaming.**

With this understanding, it's a little easier to see why children have so many nightmares. Hasn't there always been an attack on God's original, perfect design for our bodies? The enemy tries his best to sever this powerful line of communication at the very youngest age possible to prevent children from receiving messages from God through dreams.

However, God created us for dreaming. Dreaming is His divine plan for our lives. He knows what's best for us. He formed us in our mother's womb. Psalm 139:14 says we are fearfully and wonderfully made. God knew what the absolute perfect design would be for our bodies, and part of His masterful design was the ability to dream.

I hear people say all the time, "Well, I don't dream." A more accurate statement would be "I don't remember my dreams." We have to dream each night or our mental health becomes compromised.

I read a report years ago that said a study was conducted on a certain number of subjects who were consistently awakened right before entering R.E.M. After two to three nights of this, the subjects became mentally unstable and were showing signs of nervous breakdowns. The scientists concluded that our bodies require us to enter into a state of dreaming. So whether you realize it or not … you *are* dreaming every night!

Knowing that God created your child to dream with Him each night should get you very excited! It's part of your child's design to be a dreamer. It was His good pleasure to create us for dreaming and we're about to explore some reasons why — so keep reading!

Family Activation!

★ Read Genesis chapter one as a family. Talk about God's perfect design in everything He created. Share with your children that He created their bodies perfectly and dreams are a part of that perfect design. Read Psalm 139:14 to them.

★ Pray together and thank God for how He created your bodies. Thank Him for choosing to speak to you at night through dreams. Ask God to release dreams to your family and the ability to remember the dreams He gives you. Go to bed with the expectation that your family will receive dreams from God that night.

★ When you get up in the morning, make a breakfast date as a family and discuss the dreams you had. It would be fun to create a family dream book where everyone can draw pictures and write down words that remind them of dreams they've had. See if there's one particular message that God seems to be speaking to your entire family.

Chapter 2
But Why Dreams?

The question a lot of people want to know is, "But why dreams?" I mean, if God really wants me to know something, why doesn't He just come out and say it in plain English?!

I believe there are several very good reasons why God chose dreams as a way of speaking to us. First of all, let me paint a picture of the average American lifestyle. Get up way earlier than you wish you had to, skip breakfast as you rush out the door, work, grab a few bites of lunch as you maneuver your way through the drive-through, work, lots of coffee, work some more … more drive-through on your way to kid's baseball game, home, throw something together for supper, laundry, TV, crash, repeat.

I'm not saying there was no time for hearing God. However, I would venture to guess there wasn't a huge amount of time carved out of your day for hearing God's voice and receiving instructions and advice about life. When you lie down at night and you enter into a state of dreaming, I imagine God is saying, "OK … now we can *finally* talk!" All the day's activities come to an end, your mind and body are at rest, and finally all is quiet. It becomes the perfect atmosphere for conversation.

Assuming you are getting at least six to eight hours of sleep per night, that is a huge chunk of time where God has your undivided attention! God will not let such valuable time slip by without using it to speak to you about your life and destiny. Maybe He will give you warnings about the future that will guide you in the right direction. If you can't find a solution to a problem, He will use dreams to give you practical advice and impart wisdom to you. He uses dreams to train you to: deal with things you're going to encounter in life, operate in your gifts, or defeat the enemy's plans for you. Not all dreams are for you; He also uses dreams to show you how to intercede for others. Some dreams are for healing relationships. There are countless things that God might be trying to tell you in a dream, if you have ears to hear.

Psalm 16:7 says, "I will praise the Lord, who counsels me; even at night my heart instructs me." The Passion translation of this verse says, "For your whispers in the night give me wisdom, showing me what to do next." This verse tells us God is giving our heart instructions at night, He's whispering wisdom in our ears, and He's showing us what to do next. Dreams are a one-on-one private counseling session with God.

There is a demonstration with money that I do with kids when I teach them about dreams. I tell them that counseling sessions average between $100-$200 an hour. So if they are getting eight hours of sleep, they are getting up to $1600 worth of free counseling sessions every night. That's $48,000 a month and $576,000 a year of the finest counseling on this planet and they don't have to pay a dime for it!

> **Every night you enter a time where all of the day's activities come to a standstill, and you can receive the wise counseling of the Holy Spirit through dreams.**

If you have a belief system that dreams don't really mean anything, you're going to miss all those nightly nuggets of wisdom the Holy Spirit is offering.

Having a quiet time to talk to us is one reason God uses dreams to speak to us, let's look at another. Once again, we're going to look at the science of dreaming to help us gain insight. An article titled "Five Actual Facts About Dreams" explains what happens to our brains when we dream. [d] Here is what it said:

"Your limbic system (hippocampus and fornix — the wormy tangle in the middle of your brain) is the primary control center for your emotions, and it becomes especially active during your dreams. This explains why dreams are so emotionally charged. Meanwhile, the dorsolateral prefrontal cortex, which controls logic and rationality, is practically dormant. This explains why you can dream of yourself marrying Hugh Griffith in an cosmonaut suit and be like, "Can we have the guests throw sand instead of Cracker Jacks, Hughie? Birds tend to choke on the prizes."

There are other articles that support the finding of this one. The conclusion is that the logical part of our brain is almost completely inactive during dreams. It's as if God shuts down our ability to say that something is impossible, so he can show us anything He wants and we won't argue with Him about it.

For example, what if God said to you during the day, "Let's go flying together!" Your logic would immediately begin to argue with you. And logic would win out! You'd end up shaking it off as just a silly thought that popped into your head, and move on with your day.

Then that night you have a dream that you are flying. Why? Because God can take you places and do things with you in a dream that He can't do with you during the day. You can go on adventures together that defy logic and *actually* seem quite normal to you in the dream!

Not only that, you knew what it *felt* like to fly in the dream— how your body felt in the air and all the sensations you experienced. Have you ever wondered how it's possible to know what something feels like in a dream that you've never experienced before in real life? Yet you can experience them in a dream as if you've done them before!

Remember how the scientific findings show that the primary control of your emotions is especially active during a dream? This is why dreams can be so emotional. Have you ever had a dream and the emotions you felt in the dream were so real that even after you woke up, you could still feel those same emotions hours later?

God heightens our emotions in a dream to draw us in and engage us deeply with the dream. This is how God designed our brains to make dreaming real to us and draw our emotions into the experience.

I've had dreams that I woke up from and it took me half the day to convince myself it was just a dream. It felt so real to me that you *couldn't* convince me that it didn't actually happen. Most adults are so good at being "adults" that we tend to overuse our logic, limit the creative side of our brain, and suppress deep emotions. God in His infinite wisdom designed our brains so we could enter into an experience through dreams that would bypass all that logic, activate all that pent up creativity, and draw out our true emotions. What an amazing design!

I believe there is an example of this in Genesis when Jacob dreamed about the ladder that went to heaven, and he saw angels ascending and descending. Genesis 28:16 says that after Jacob woke up from his dream he said, "Surely the Lord was in this place, and I was unaware of it."

I believe God bypassed Jacob's thinker. Maybe God knew that Jacob would have a hard time believing the message that He needed to deliver to him; therefore, He spoke to Jacob in a dream because Jacob wouldn't argue with God about it!

Another reason why I believe God designed us for dreaming is because it's a time for us to heal. Your body actually repairs itself while you're sleeping. That's why when you're sick your body cries out for rest. The couch becomes your new best friend and your pillow your soul mate. There's just no fighting it — your body says, "Sleep so I can heal!" And you know what? It's usually right! You wake up in the morning feeling tremendously better after a good night of sleep.

Your body isn't the only thing that heals at night. Have you ever gone to bed with your mind feeling totally exhausted? When you wake up in the morning, your mind feels refreshed and ready to take on the day! Of course, for some of us, our brains still don't fully function before noon but it's certainly better than when we went to bed!

That's also why you'll hear people say, "I'll sleep on it," when they need to make important decisions. It's because after a good night of sleep, your mind is clearer and it's easier to make decisions. Your mind is healing while you're sleeping.

But here's the thing — we're made up of three parts…body, mind, and spirit. John 4:24 tells us that God is spirit. Genesis 2:7 tells us that God breathed His Spirit into us, creating us to be spirits as well. God communicates with us Spirit to spirit. Dreams are a spiritual God communicating with our spirits.

So if God made a plan for our bodies and minds to become refreshed at night, don't you think He wants to do the same for our spirits?

> **Our spirits need to heal and be strengthened just like our bodies and minds do when we rest. Dreams are a way for God to speak to our spirits about areas we need to heal and grow in.**

If we're paying attention to our dreams, they can become very healing for us.

There's one last reason I want to talk about for why God chose dreams as a way of communicating with us. Remember at the beginning when I said people ask why He can't just speak to them in plain English? It's actually His grace and mercy that He doesn't!

If Jesus were to show up in your room right now and clearly tell you what He wants you to know, you would have a VERY high level of accountability to do what He asks you to do. There's no room for error when Jesus uses plain English. However, if God uses symbols in a dream to convey a message to you, and you get it wrong—there's grace for that!

Let's say God wants you to deliver a message to your co-worker. He speaks to you in a dream and conveys the message to you through symbols. You aren't positive what the message is that you're supposed to deliver, so you spend time praying about the meaning of the dream. In this case, God extends you a level of grace if you don't deliver the message exactly right.

But if Jesus spoke to you face to face and told you the exact message you were to deliver, now there's no room for error! The higher the level of "knowing," the more accountable you become. Now aren't you glad that He speaks in dreams?!

Family Activation!

★ Now it's time for your family to dream like Jacob did when he saw a ladder ascending to heaven. First, read the story together of Jacob's dream in Genesis 28:10-20.

★ Next, have everyone close their eyes. Lead your family in imagining the following things, pausing between each statement to allow time for the imagination to take over:

> Imagine a ladder that leads to heaven. Now begin to climb the ladder. When you get to the top, Jesus will be there waiting for you. Ask Jesus to show you around. Next, ask Jesus for a gift that you are supposed to bring back down the ladder and release on the earth. Come back down the ladder and share with each other what you saw.

★ A family journal would be a good way to record everything you hear and see together as a family. Many times this activity will reveal to the parents a calling their child has, so it's good to write down what everyone saw/experienced. It's also a good idea to write the date you did the activity in the journal and the ages of the children.

Chapter 3

Imagine That!

If you did the "Family Activation" in chapter two, then you were using a very powerful tool that God uses to speak to you, called your imagination! The imagination plays a strong role in children's dreams, so it's worth dedicating a whole chapter to it.

Try this. Close your eyes and imagine yourself at your favorite vacation spot, eating your favorite foods, surrounded by your favorite people, and then open your eyes back up when you're done.

Welcome back! How was your vacation? Hard to come back, wasn't it?! Unless, of course, your favorite vacation spot was a deserted, tropical island that suddenly got overrun by monkey lords right before the tsunami of the century hit. Oh, wait … that's my imagination gone wild, not yours! Let's reign it back in. The only reason you are able to close your eyes and see any pictures at all is because God gave you a built-in picture board in your mind called your imagination. When I teach kids, I refer to their imagination as a whiteboard in their minds. It's a tool God gives each one of us in order to communicate messages to us.

Children are naturally tuned into this special way of communicating with God. It's only when adults start telling them things like, "It was *only* your imagination" or "Wow you *certainly* have a wild imagination, don't you?" (as they roll their eyes) that kids start to develop an altered view of their imagination. This leads to a perception that as they grow up, they should also outgrow their childish imaginations.

However, we were designed with an imagination just like we were designed with the ability to dream. Our imaginations have been in place ever since the very beginning, because it's part of God's perfect design for us. We wouldn't even have the ability see pictures in our minds if the Creator hadn't coded it into our very DNA. Clearly it was meant to be used!

So, at what point do you think God wants you to outgrow this gift? Did He intend for your imagination to be turned off at some point or reduced down to only what seems fitting for an adult? We haven't outgrown our need for other parts of our design — like eyes for seeing. Have you ever heard somebody say, "You know I used to use my eyes when I was little but as I grew up I really didn't see a need for them anymore so now I walk around with my eyes shut."

OK ... so maybe that's a little extreme, but do you at least see my point? Our imagination is part of our design (just like our eyes) and it was never meant to be outgrown. Maybe being all "grown-up-y" isn't all it's cracked up to be! Maybe we need to stop walking around with the eyes of our imagination closed. It's time to open up to the world of possibilities in our imagination and see what messages God has been writing there, waiting for us to see again. So what does all this have to do with dreams? Everything!

> **Your imagination is like a bridge between the waking and nighttime hours. Everything you take in during the day has the potential to go over that bridge and into your dreams to affect them.**

You have to guard your imagination like Swiss guards guarding the pope ... nothing gets through without your approval!

That's why it's so important that you are vigilant about what your children are taking in during the day, since they are so good at using their imaginations. Everything they are watching, reading, listening, playing, etc., can have a profound impact on their dreams at night as those images march over that bridge. A great number of nightmares in children could be prevented if guards were put in place.

As a parent, this takes a lot of discernment because what may bother one child has no affect on another. You have to pray and discern for each child what they can handle. Something that seems innocent enough to you, could be affecting your child's dreams because their imagination is more active than yours.

Of course, there are some things that should be avoided all together. Let's take violent video games as an example. A child plays video games with very graphic content. Next, the child begins to imagine things during the day that are violent in nature. Before you know it, the child begins to have very graphic and violent dreams.

What the child took in during the day was the violent game. The imagination that absorbed all that content became a bridge that allowed the violence to cross over into their dreams. Not every single thing a child takes in during the day will show up in a dream, but I believe everything at least has the potential to.

A lot of adults are quite sensitive in the same way a child would be. Personally, I have always had a very active imagination. I guess I missed the memo that I was supposed to outgrow it! For years I had to guard my mind because if I saw it … I dreamed it! If I went to a funeral, I refused to look at the person in the casket because I knew that dead person would show up in my dreams. I even avoided movies like *Lord of the Rings* because strong imagery would have a profound affect on my dreams.

In my case, I was overprotective of my mind out of fear. I was afraid if I saw something unpleasant, it would come to haunt me in my imagination and then in my dreams. My fear stemmed from recurring nightmares as a child. In order to protect myself from having nightmares, I avoided everything that even had a remote possibility of affecting my imagination and, therefore, my dreams.

Thankfully in recent years God has delivered me from this fear. I can now see negative images and I know that it doesn't have the power to affect my dreams. It doesn't mean I watch anything I want; I still guard my mind and use discernment. The difference is that if I happen to see something, I no longer have the fear and the anticipation that it's going to haunt my dreams at night.

Even though I no longer fear what I see and how it will affect my dreams, I still am vigilant about keeping my imagination clean. There's a demonstration I do with kids when I teach them about keeping their imaginations clean. I tell them their imagination is like a giant whiteboard in their minds. It's a place where God puts pictures, colors, movies, or anything else He wants to show them.

Our imagination starts off nice, white, and clean (as I'm showing the kids the clean whiteboard) but yucky stuff can get on it. I ask the kids for examples of yucky stuff that can get in their imagination. As they tell me things like "bad T.V. shows," "bad music," "curse words," "violent games," "books about witchcraft," etc., I begin to write those phrases in big, black letters on the clean whiteboard. Before they know it, the whiteboard has a bunch of yucky, black phrases all over it.

Next I tell them that God wants to show them a picture using their imagination (as I try to draw a picture over top of all the black words). It's not that they can't see any parts of the picture but they can only see glimpses of it. They are only guessing what it might be because they can't clearly see it through all the black marks that were made.

The good news for kids (and the good news for me when God was delivering me from fear) is: the Holy Spirit has a giant eraser! I tell the kids that He can erase all those black words off their whiteboards, a.k.a. imaginations. I then erase the whiteboard with an eraser that says "Holy Spirit" on it and show them how nice and clean it is again. Finally, I draw the same picture I did the first time but now they can clearly see what it is!

Keeping our imaginations clean is not a one-time event. We live in a world where it's really, *really* easy to pick up yucky stuff on our whiteboards. Thankfully, we can ask the Holy Spirit to erase things from our whiteboards as often as we need Him to.

This has been a tremendous help to me, even as an adult. When I see something I really wish I hadn't seen, I simply imagine the Holy Spirit with His giant eraser wiping my imagination clean again. Then I feel released and I have no fear of that image showing up in my dreams.

Philippians 4:8 tells us what we can replace those images with. It says, "Finally, brothers and sisters, whatever is true, whatever is noble, whatever is right, whatever is pure, whatever is lovely, whatever is admirable — if anything is excellent or praiseworthy — think about such things. Whatever you have learned or received or heard from me, or seen in me — put it into practice. And the God of peace will be with you. And the peace of God, which transcends all understanding, will guard your hearts and your minds in Christ Jesus."

Christ will guard our minds (and imaginations)

and give us peace. Our part is to choose to think about things that are true, right, pure, excellent, etc. When we guard our thoughts like this, we are also guarding our dreams at night.

I believe as parents we need to be teaching our children how to make the hard choices about protecting their imaginations. For example, even if everyone around them is watching or reading something they know they shouldn't be, they have to make the decision to walk away.

> **We can't always be with our kids to make sure their imaginations are protected. But when kids are taught about the role of their imagination and the importance of guarding it, they can make wise choices on their own.**

They will soon learn that those things are not worth messing up their whiteboards, because it makes it more difficult to hear God. Psalm 101:3 says, "I will set no wicked thing before my eyes; it shall not stick to me." Some versions say, "I will have no part in it." We need to teach our kids to make the tough choices and say, "I will have no part in it!" Sometimes the tough choices will be the parents that have to say, "*You* will have not part in it!" It's takes boldness but it will be so worth it when your child can clearly see the pictures that God paints in their dreams and imaginations!

Family Activation!

★ If you have a whiteboard at home, review this chapter with your kids and teach them how their imagination is like a whiteboard. If you don't have a whiteboard, a blank piece of white paper would also work. Discuss possible things they might have gotten on their whiteboards that shouldn't be there.

★ As a family, close your eyes and ask the Holy Spirit to show you what the whiteboards in your minds look like. Ask Him to show you any black marks that have gotten there. Then, ask the Holy Spirit to come along with His giant eraser and erase any black marks that are there — leaving you with a nice, clean imagination.

★ Now that all of your whiteboards (imaginations) are clean, ask the Holy Spirit to draw any pictures He wants there. Share as a family what you saw and record everything in your family journal.

Chapter 4
Vivid Visions

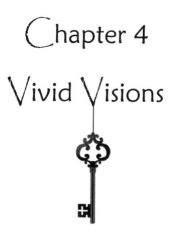

Along with very active imaginations, children are also known for their vivid visions. Because of this, I thought I would take some time to talk about what visions are and how they are different than dreams. Most people say the main difference between the two is that dreams are symbolic and visions are more literal.

Wikipedia states, "A vision is something seen in a dream, trance or religious practice, especially a supernatural appearance that usually conveys a revelation. Visions generally have more clarity than dreams." I tell kids that visions are like movies in their minds. Sometimes when people see visions, they will see a movie screen appear before them and the vision will play out on the screen. You can see visions with your eyes open or closed, and generally they happen when you're awake. On the contrary, dreams are almost exclusively during sleep when your eyes are closed.

There are several accounts in the Bible that we can read about to help us understand the nature of visions. Acts chapter nine is the story of Saul's conversion. Saul was suddenly blinded by a light from heaven on his way to Damascus. The Lord wanted to know why Saul was persecuting Him. Saul asked the Lord what he needed to do next, so he was given instructions to go to the city. After Saul was led to Damascus by his traveling companions, the Lord gave His disciple, Ananias, a vision about Saul.

Acts 9:10-12 says, "In Damascus there was a disciple name Ananias. The Lord called to him in a vision. The Lord told him, "Go to the house of Judas on Straight Street and ask for a man from Tarsus named Saul, for he is praying. In a vision he has seen a man named Ananias come and place his hands on him to restore his sight."

These verses tell us that God not only gave Ananias a vision telling him to go lay hands on Saul, but He also gave Saul a vision as well. Saul had a vision that a man was going to come and pray for him and then his sight would be restored. And, that's exactly what happened in Acts 9:17-18. We learn from this story that visions can be very literal.

An interesting thing to note is that Saul was blind when he had the vision. Therefore, we know that he wasn't seeing the vision with his physical eyes but rather a vision in his mind while he was awake. Frequently when I see visions, it's during times of worship at church or at home. I close my eyes and I begin to see pictures and movies being played out. Some people see pictures or movies as clearly as if they were actually there in the natural. When I see pictures, it's a "knowing." I don't actually see the picture, but I have a deep knowing of what the picture is. That knowing is just as clear to me as if I were seeing an actual picture.

Another example of a vision can be found in Genesis 15:1-21. It says, "After these things the word of the Lord came to Abraham in a vision, saying, "Do not be afraid, Abram, I am your shield, your exceedingly great reward." Verse five says, "Then He brought him outside and said, "Look now toward the heaven, and count the stars if you are able to number them." And He said to him, "So shall your descendants be."

In Abraham's vision, he was wide awake, and God was having him move and go places during the vision. This is called an open vision. During an open vision, we can be walking around as the vision is being played out right before our eyes. You can also read about another vision like this in Acts 10:9-13. Peter fell into a trance and saw a vision. During the vision, God instructed him to get up and go do something.

You can also have a vision in a dream. Visions are not limited to *only* when you're awake. Daniel 7:1-2 says, "Daniel had a dream and visions of his head while on his bed." One time I was having a dream and all of a sudden I looked out a big window and a movie began to play out. I knew what I was seeing was a vision within my dream. Usually when you're seeing a vision in a dream, the vision is being played out on a T.V. screen, through a window, or perhaps a picture on a wall. Those are clues that you're having a vision in a dream.

I have a friend that has frequent visions. I'm more of a dreamer, so I asked her for advice about how to receive more visions. She told me the key is not to seek visions. Focus on God. When we focus on God, visions will be the natural overflow. I think this is why so many kids have visions. They aren't seeking to have them; they seem to happen so naturally for them. Kids are so in tune to the spirit realm without even trying that visions and imaginations are easier for them than most adults.

At times, children can seem frightened by the visions they are seeing, because the vision appears to be so real to them. It's a normal reaction for them to feel afraid when they start seeing them. Zechariah saw a vision in the book of Luke and it says, "He was startled and was gripped with fear." But an angel told

Zechariah not to be afraid. Abraham also must have felt afraid in his open vision, because the first thing God said to him was, "Do not be afraid, Abram. I am Your shield, your exceedingly great reward." (Genesis 15:1)

I think it's important to let our kids know that it's normal to feel scared sometimes when they see a vision. They need to know that God will give them peace if it's a vision from Him. If they are seeing visions that are very upsetting and they have no peace, then it might not be from God. They can ask Jesus to take over their thoughts, be their shield, and give them peace.

Even though some visions are literal, a lot have symbolism just like dreams. If a child says they see angels during a worship time in church, it's likely they are literally seeing angels. However, if a child says they see a vision of a waterfall coming down and pouring over the people, this would be symbolic. Symbols in a vision can be interpreted just like symbols in a dream. I'll talk more about symbolism in chapters eight and nine.

I would highly encourage parents that have kids seeing visions to talk to them about what they are seeing. Don't brush it off as nothing but a wild imagination. Kids *really* are seeing things that most adults don't have a grid for understanding. By downplaying or ignoring what they are seeing, we are slowly stifling a valuable gift inside them.

Family Activation!

★ After talking to your kids about visions, tell them that having a vision from God is like having on a super, powerful pair of glasses. The glasses help you to see things that you never would have seen otherwise.

★ Before starting this activity, pray with your family and ask God to release visions to each of you. Next, have everyone close their eyes and pause between each of the following statements:

> Imagine yourself in a room with Jesus. Jesus is sitting in a chair and there's a table beside Him with a pair of glasses on it. When you put on the glasses, you'll be able to see visions. Ask Jesus to hand you the glasses and then put them on. Once you have the glasses on, look around.

★ Share the visions God gave each of you. Remember to write down what everyone saw in your family journal.

Chapter 5
Reasons For Nightmares

If you've ever had a child with recurring nightmares, you know they are no joke! I think every parent who has spent the night on their child's floor after a bad dream, wishes they had the power to make nightmares stop for good. Instead, they find themselves feeling more helpless than ever.

When you read the statistics, it's not surprising to hear that so many kids are having nightmares. One source says up to 50% of children between the ages of three and six are having consistent nightmares. [e] Another one says nearly 70% of children ten and under are having nightmares. [f]

It begs the question, "Why are so many kids having nightmares?" I believe at least one of the reasons stems from what we talked about in chapter one. Whether you realize it right now or not, your enemy already knows how powerful dreams are and he will start as early as possible to sever that powerful line of communication your child was born with. And, Satan doesn't care if your child is ten years old or six months old; his only goal is to cause enough fear in your child that they try to shut off the gift of dreaming.

So, how can a child turn off their dreams? The child makes an inner vow that says, "Dreams are bad, dreams are scary, and I don't want to dream anymore." The child might not even consciously know that they made a vow. However, there's something inside them that decided if this is what dreaming is like, then they didn't want to dream anymore. I have had children come up to me and tell me that dreams are too scary and they don't like to dream anymore. And guess what? They can turn off their dreams with a vow like that.

Numbers 30:2 says, "If a man vow a vow unto the LORD, or swear an oath to bind his soul with a bond; he shall not break his word, he shall do according to all that proceedeth out of his mouth." Sometimes we make inner vows to bind our souls because there are places we just won't allow ourselves to go. If dreams are too dark and scary, kids can essentially block off their ability to dream.

I just want to say that as a parent, do not come into agreement with that kind of vow. If your child is saying things like that, you might not know all the answers about how to help them, but silence sometimes is a form of agreement. Speak the opposite, pray with them, and remind them that God's design for dreams is good, and this is not part of His design for them.

This is not unique to kids; many adults have blocked off their ability to dream as well. I believe this happens quite often when men and women who have seen war come back and begin to experience nightmares. They shut down their ability to dream so they can no longer experience the pain of the memory. Any kind of traumatic event that causes recurring dreams or nightmares can cause you to relive things that you simply don't want to. The only problem with shutting off your dreams is, it's also blocking off the good dreams—including the dreams that have the potential to heal.

Even if a child or adult makes this inner vow, I believe that God will still speak to them in their dreams. However, it's going to be a little more challenging to receive a dream from God if they have a belief system that dreaming is a bad or negative experience.

Remember, dreams are part of our design; it's in our DNA to be dreamers. God uses dreams to communicate powerful messages to us. Satan has always tried to hijack God's original, perfect design for us. So

Satan will try his best to shut down your children's dreams through dark experiences at night.

I heard John Thomas from Streams International say that if a child makes it through the first seven to eight years without shutting off their dreams, they usually go through another round when they are teenagers. This time the enemy uses nightmares as a way of luring teens into a fascination with the dark side.

> **Kids are hungry for supernatural experiences. If the home and church aren't giving kids opportunities to experience healthy supernatural encounters, they will be lured into what the world is offering them.**

Dark dreams give teens supernatural experiences they are longing for. We need to be giving our kids an outlet for healthy supernatural experiences with the real deal before they fall for a counterfeit!

If you don't know how to develop an atmosphere for your children to have healthy supernatural encounters, there are resources available to help you. One resource is Kids in Ministry International. KIMI is dedicated to helping parents raise a generation of kids that know who their God is, and will never have to fall for the counterfeit because they know the real deal. Of course the best place to start is always seeking the Holy Spirit for guidance.

Besides Satan trying to shut down the gift of dreaming, there are other reasons why a child might be having nightmares. One of them we already covered in chapter three, which is an unsanctified imagination. If you're child is having nightmares because of something inappropriate they watched, read, or played, then those things need removed from the home. Ask the Holy Spirit to cleanse their mind and pray for a release of His dreams upon them. This will usually put an end to their nightmares.

I'm not going to go into great detail but here's a list of some other reasons why a child might be having nightmares:

- Poor diet
- Medications
- Illnesses
- Changes in hormones
- Traumas such as: death of someone close to them, an accident they were involved in, divorce of their parents, abuses they have suffered, etc.
- An item was brought into the house that has witchcraft or a demonic presence attached to it
- The home is filled with anger, depression, fear, arguing, anxiety, inappropriate spiritual warfare, etc.

Another reason a child might be having nightmares is because of a generational or deliberate sin in one of the parents. It's a hard thing for a parent to face, but the fact is our choice to sin *does* have an affect on our children's dreams.

God started teaching me this concept about a year ago. Adults were telling me about nightmares they used to have as a child. The scenes and scenarios in the dreams they had never seen in real life. They had no idea where the ideas they were dreaming about were coming from. Some of the dreams were even leading the child into the same perversion they were seeing in their dreams. Then years later as an adult, they would find out that one of their parents was involved in the very act they saw in their dreams.

I don't claim to understand how this works. I just know that when we sin, it opens a door of attack in our homes. These attacks can have a profound affect on our children and their dreams. As parents, we have to close the doors of sin in our own lives to make sure it's not affecting our children.

This doesn't mean that we have to be perfect as parents. We all have areas we struggle in and are working through. I don't believe that when we are working through issues, seeking God, and repenting that our children are vulnerable to nightmares. What I'm talking about is deliberate and willful sin. Willful sin leaves the door wide open for the enemy to come into our homes and affect the entire atmosphere. Often we are so blind to it that we choose to do nothing about it.

If you are not deliberately sinning and your children are having nightmares for any of the reasons we've talked about, then there is something you can do. It's called using your AUTHORITY!

> **Parents already have all the authority they need over the enemy and his scheme to disrupt your children's dreams at night.**

This is the way I describe it to parents with kids having nightmares. Let's say a burglar breaks into your home at night and sneaks back to your children's rooms to assault them. What would you do? Most dads I know would be grabbing their gun, running the guy down, and beating him up while mom is on the phone with the police! You have all the authority you need in the eyes of the law to justify these actions.

Nightmares are spiritual assaults from a burglar on your children. The way you would react to a burglar in the natural is the same way you should react to one in the spiritual. And just like in the natural, you have been given all the authority you need in the heavenly courtroom to justify your actions. So use the spiritual authority you've been given to pull out your weapon, run the devil out, and call on the policeman with the ultimate authority—God!

As a parent, you have to have a no-tolerance attitude when it comes to nightly assaults against your children. If you aren't sure how to use your authority, do a biblical study on authority. Matthew chapter eight is one example. The Roman centurion understood how authority worked, and because of, that Jesus was amazed by his faith.

You have been given authority in your children's lives and what happens in your home. Satan hates authority and he hates when parents use their authority to disarm his attacks against them. Remember that our authority has been granted to us by Christ. It's His name that carries the ultimate authority. Use the name of Jesus to send the devil packing!

Parents are not the only ones that carry authority. *Every* believer has been given authority over the devil. If your child is a believer, they have authority as well. That means we should not only be using *our* authority in the home, but also teaching our kids about the authority that *they* carry. Kids can use their authority in a dream to change the outcome. I'll cover this in detail in the next chapter.

Family Activation!

★ Practicing something together in the natural realm can activate a shift in the spiritual realm. For fun, take turns pretending that one of you is a robber and one of you is a policeman. Have the robber pretend he's sneaking into the room. Everyone in the family can pretend to call the police. Then have the designated policeman come out and arrest the robber.

★ Explain to your kids that this is what nightmares are like. Tell them the burglar is like Satan and the police office is like God. Remind them that they can call on God anytime they need Him to arrest Satan for disturbing their dreams.

★ If you want to take it even further, print off a sheriff's badge for your kids to color and leave by their beds at night, as a reminder that God is the ultimate authority and He's always with them.

Chapter 6
Warriors In Training

I remember one time my pastor told me that Native Americans would allow their children to play with weapons of war such as tomahawks, bow and arrows, knives, and spears. He said the reason they allowed the children to play with such weapons was because they would become familiar with how the weapons felt in their hands, how the weapons would react during playtimes, and how they needed to respond to the weapons. The daily use would allow the weapons to become second nature to the children.

When the children were actually old enough to need the weapons, they were already skilled in how to use them. No further training was needed because they had been training to become warriors all their lives and didn't even know it.

I can't think of a better picture for the spiritual training of our children. There's been a battle taking place around our children ever since they were born. Frequently, we aren't aware of the battle ourselves, so we neglect to train our children how to use the weapons of their warfare. Or we think they are too young so we wait until they are older to start training them.

The Native Americans knew that if they waited until the children were older to begin the training, it could cost them their lives during a battle, because they were just beginning to learn how to use their weapons. I believe there is something we can learn from the Native Americans when it comes to when and how we train our children to use the spiritual weapons they've been given.

There's another reason why children have nightmares that we haven't talked about yet, and it has to do with this very thing. It's because dark dreams are for training our children how to use their spiritual weapons. Jesus doesn't always remove every presence of evil from affecting our lives because how would we learn how to use the weapons of our warfare? How would we learn to use the authority that we've been given over the power of the enemy?

Luke 10:19 says, "Behold, I give you the authority … over all the power of the enemy, and nothing shall by any means hurt you." This verse tells us that we have already been given authority over all the power of the enemy—including in our dreams. We could read the verse like this, "Behold, I give *your children* the authority over all the power of the enemy *in their dreams* and nothing shall by any means hurt them."

> **Your children have been given power to overcome the enemy in their dreams. A solider sharpens his skills during a battle. Dreams are the same way. Sometimes children have dark dreams because they need to learn how to use the tools they've been given to fight their battles and come out victorious. Jesus isn't giving them the dark dreams, but He might be allowing them to go through for training purposes.**

Nightmares are often thought of as completely out of our control. We are just simply victims of whatever is unfolding in the dream. When we teach our children how to use their authority in a dream to change the outcome, we are taking them from being a victim *of* their dreams to an overcomer *in* their dreams. In this way we are training our little warriors how to use the weapons they've been given.

Did you notice I said IN their dreams? Children can use the authority they have to change the outcome of their dreams *while* they are still dreaming. When my husband isn't so sure about something I've said, he has a signature "one-eyebrow raise." I'm wondering how many eyebrows I just raised with that statement, so let me explain to you what I mean.

Let me start off by saying I do not have chapter and verse proof of what I'm about to say. It is, however, based on spiritual principals and personal experience — not just my own, but the experiences of many others as well. It's up to you to read and discern whether you feel this is right for your family or not. The goal is to share with you one method I have had the most success with for overcoming nightmares.

One powerful weapon children have been given to change their dreams is Jesus. During my dream workshops, I teach children how to find Jesus in their dreams. Hebrews 1:5 tells us that Jesus is always with us and He'll never forsake us. Jesus is with us even in our darkest dreams, if we know how to find Him.

Since most of us have never seen Jesus face to face, we don't know what He looks like. Therefore, when we have a dream about Jesus, He comes in another form with which we can identify. Since Matthew 28:18 says that all authority on heaven and earth has been given to Jesus, it's very common for Him to show up in our dreams as someone that we identify as being an authority figure.

For kids, Jesus often looks like a police officer, principal, fireman, superhero, etc. For adults, He often comes in the form of our earthly dad or pastor. Once we learn to recognize what form Jesus comes in our dreams, we can begin to call on Him for help.

I had a mom tell me her son dreamed about a wolf chasing him. She said off in the distance he saw woods and a hunter standing there with a gun. I told her the hunter was Jesus and He was there to shoot the wolf for her son. I also told her that if he ever had that dream again, all he had to do was call on the hunter and He would come and shoot the wolf for him.

You can also bring Jesus into your dreams by using your imagination. Here's where the imagination comes in that we talked about earlier! If you are being chased by a car, imagine a tow truck driver comes and tows the car away. If a person is chasing you, imagine a police officer tackling the bad guy and putting him in jail. Is your dream too dark? Imagine a giant light switch on the wall and watch the darkness flee as the light floods your dream. In this way, you are bringing Jesus into your dreams to help you overcome whatever bad thing is happening.

You might be wondering how all this is even possible! Just by my telling you that it is, is the first step. Everything that you hear and take in during the day has the potential to show up in your dreams at night. If you carry the knowledge with you that you can change your dreams, you'll have access to that knowledge while you're in a dream. Kids can use this tool a lot easier than adults because they have less logic to by-pass!

Now, all of this doesn't mean you and your kids will have the power to change every dream you have. This method is used for dark dreams to overcome the plans of the enemy against you. God will let you know when you have the ability to change your dream by making you aware in the dream that you can change it.

Here's an example of how I became aware that I could change a dream. One time I had a dream that I was standing in my living room looking out our big picture window. All of a sudden these dark waves like an ocean starting rolling in toward our house. I suddenly became aware that I was dreaming and I knew that I could change the outcome of the dream. I went to the front door, opened it up, and commanded the waves to recede — which they did!

I used the authority that God had given me over the plans of the enemy to change the outcome of the dream. I could have woken up from the dream thinking something really bad was going to happen to our home. Instead, I woke up in peace because I saw that whatever plan the enemy had — it receded back!

> **Using our authority in a dream will be the difference between waking up in fear or waking up in victory!**

There's another fun way we can teach our kids how to use their authority in a dream. For years I was mentored by a Streams Ministries graduate. He told me at Streams they would train kids to change their dreams by using their favorite games and superheroes. Once I heard about it, I started using it to teach kids and found it to be very effective.

Here's the idea. Every movie or game has some element of good guy versus bad guy. The good guys have weapons they use to defeat the bad guys. You can teach your kids to use those same "good guy" weapons in their dreams to defeat whatever bad thing is happening to them.

Let's say your child loves playing Mario Kart. During the races, you have certain powers you can use to slow down everyone else around you. For example, you can strike your opponents with lightning and make them tiny, you can throw banana peels at them, or splatter the screen so they can't see where they're going.

Do you see where I'm going with this one? Yep, your children can use all those powers in a dream to stop their bad guys as well. They can strike them with lightning so they are too tiny to chase them, throw banana peels down so they can't run, or splatter them with something that blinds them. All you have to do is talk to your children about their favorite games and find out what weapons they have for defeating the bad guys. Then tell your kids that they can use those same weapons in their dreams as well!

The same method can be used with superheroes. One time I asked a boy who his favorite superhero was—he said, "Batman!" I asked him what the people used when they needed Batman's help. He told me they would throw a bat signal up into the sky and then Batman would come to their rescue. I told him the next time he needed help in a dream to throw a bat signal up into the sky and help would be on the way!

This might take a little creative thinking, but it's one of the most powerful tools I've ever encountered for overcoming nightmares. It might feel silly at first, but there is something that is activated when our spirits rise up and take over a dream that the enemy meant to harm us.

A lot of dark dreams have to do with learning to activate the authority that we carry because dreams are essentially a training ground. Dreams are a safe place for us to practice using our authority. Things will happen in our dream first, and then the natural will follow our dream. If we conquer something in a dream, we can conquer it the waking hours. In this way, dreams are the training ground for what happens in the natural.

If your child is having recurring dark dreams but they are having trouble changing them, have them start to imagine while they are still awake how they're going to change their dreams. As they are going to sleep, have them think about what they might do if a bad guy shows up in a dream. Just processing the dream like this in the waking hours is going to have a huge impact in their dreams.

One of the most helpful verses I have found for kids is Psalm 91:4-6. In the passion translation it says, "His massive arms are wrapped around you, protecting you. His arms of faithfulness are a shield keeping you from harm. You will never worry about an attack of demonic forces at night nor have a fear of spirit of darkness coming against you. Don't fear a thing! Whether by night or by day, demonic danger will not trouble you, nor will the powers of evil launched against you."

I would recommend going over this verse with your children. When they lay down at night remind them that no evil thing is going to conquer them tonight. Jesus is somewhere in their dream with His protective arms ready to help them.

> **It's our job as parents to train our little warriors for the battle over their dreams. We are putting tools in their hands that will take them from fear and defeat to peace and victory!**

Family Activation!

★ As a family, discuss your children's favorite games and superheroes. Talk about the bad guys and how the good guys defeat them. Discuss what weapons the good guys use. Maybe it's a light saber and some kind of blaster that defeats the bad guy. Have them describe the weapons in detail.

★ Next, teach your children how they can use these weapons in their dreams to defeat the bad guys. Discuss some dreams they've had in the past and talk about what they could have done differently or what weapons they could have used. If they like Star Wars, suggest that in their next bad dream they imagine a light saber in their hand that will defeat the bad guy.

★ Follow up with your children over the next several weeks and ask them if they've been able to change any bad dreams they might have had. If they are having trouble changing their dreams, keep making suggestions of things they can try. Pray for them that God would give them strategies for overcoming the bad guys in their dreams. Encourage them that they are learning how to use their authority.

Chapter 7
Finding The Source

I hate when I wake up in the middle of the night because I heard a bang somewhere in the house. Was someone trying to break in to steal my empire of cheesy Christmas movies? Maybe it was a mouse and all his buddies knocking over the peanut butter jar. Or perhaps it was just my son falling off the top bunk again and knocking the lamp over with his head on the way down. The point is my mind goes crazy wondering what the source of that banging sound could have been!

Figuring out the source of our children's dreams can be just as maddening. Was their dream a divine revelation from God, or just a by-product of their soul? Was a dark dream really from Satan, or was God showing them the plans of the enemy? Or maybe the dream was a manifestation of a natural fear they have. So was it soulish or demonic? Luckily for us, we have a source that we can go to that will help us discern these things.

There's not enough room in this one chapter to sufficiently talk about how to determine the source of your children's dream. It's a complicated subject matter, and to be truthful, I don't have it all figured out myself. But what I can do is share with you some *general* guidelines to get you started.

> **Job 33:15-16, "In a dream, in a vision of the night, when deep sleep falls upon men, while slumbering on their beds, then He opens the ears of men, and seals their instruction."**

Clearly from this verse we see that God is one source of dreams and visions. I John 1:5 says, "This is the message we have heard from Him and declare to you: God is light; in Him there is no darkness at all." If God is light, then we should expect that dreams from God will also be light and have bright, vibrant colors.

This is not always the case, however. Sometimes we can have a light dream that's not from God. II Corinthians 11:14 says Satan disguises himself as an angel of light. Or, we can have a dark dream that's not from Satan. It appears dark because God is showing us the plans of the enemy.

Not all dreams from God will have a soft, fuzzy feeling. Daniel 4:5 says, "I had a dream that made me afraid. As I was lying in bed, the images and visions that passed through my mind terrified me." I sort of doubt Nebuchadnezzar woke up from that dream thinking it was a bright, colorful, awesome dream from God! It also answers the question whether or not God can give dreams to unbelievers ... yes!

Daniel had dreams from God that were just as terrifying. Daniel 8:27 says, "And I, Daniel, fainted and was sick for days afterward." God was showing Daniel visions that caused him to tremble in fear.

One thing that will help us discern if a dream is from God is the fruit (or result) of the dream. Do you understand something you didn't before the dream? Do you feel like you know what God wants you to do in a certain area of your life now? Do you feel strengthened in your spirit in some way? Dreams from God result in some kind of growth, new understanding, or deepening of our relationship with Him. If we feel like we are gaining insight from the dream, that is a good clue that God was the source.

Now, let's talk about soul dreams. Our soul is our mind, will, and emotions. Sometimes it can be pretty difficult to recognize if a dream is coming from God or our own wants, needs, or emotions. There are some key questions we can ask ourselves to help us know if a dream is a product of our soul. Was the dream: something I think about often?; something I really want?; or something I often feel (negative or positive)?

The reason it can be hard to tell if a dream is from God or from your soul is because what you want is not always bad. For example, let's say you've really been wanting a new car. You can't get a new car off your mind so you've been driving past car dealerships, scouring the internet, looking in newspapers, and daydreaming about yourself riding around town in your sweet new ride.

Then one night you have a dream about getting a new car. You think this dream is from God because why wouldn't He want you to have a new car!? So you believe, and start telling people that God showed you in a dream that you're going to get a new car. Was this really a dream from God, or was it a soul dream because of your own desire for one?

It doesn't mean that God doesn't want you to have a new car, but these kinds of dreams mean you need to really pray about it first. You need to discern if it was God speaking, or your soul speaking, before you tell someone that a dream is from God.

Jeremiah 23:16 says, "They speak visions from their own minds, not from the mouth of the LORD." I Thessalonians 5:21 says "Test all things." Test yourself before claiming a dream is from God by asking yourself some of the questions I mentioned earlier, to see if this was a vision from your own mind or God speaking.

The fact is, we have leaky brains. Everything we think and experience during the day can leak into our dreams at night. Remember the imagination is like a bridge!

> **Even when we have a soul dream, God can still use the dream to speak to us about how our mind, will, and emotions are processing things around us.**

In my curriculum "Encounters in the Night," I wrote that the purpose of soul dreams is to learn something about ourselves that we might not otherwise be able to see. Your soul dream is revealing to you how you are responding to life and things around you. Take what you are learning about yourself from the soul dream and ask God how He wants you to respond to it or what you can learn from it.

In the example I gave about the car, that dream might be revealing to you that you are a little too obsessed right now with wanting a new car. A response to that dream might be to pray and release your desire for a new car to God. Let Him take care of the details so that your mind can come to a place of rest about it at night.

Soul dreams can reveal positive or negative aspects about ourselves. Your child might have soul dreams about things they are naturally afraid of, anxious about, angry about, worried about, etc. Parents and kids often perceive these types of dreams as nightmares. I'm convinced that a lot of nightmares that children think they are having are actually soul dreams.

When you are a small child, the world can feel a bit overwhelming at times. It's normal for a child to have a certain amount of fears. These fears can leak out into their dreams. This does not mean that the dream was demonic; it means the child is having a ==soul dream that is revealing a particular issue or fear in their life, and it's manifesting at night==.

This is going to take discernment for the parents to recognize the dream was a product of a negative feeling or emotion the child was having in real life that manifested in a dream. James 1:5 says, "If anyone lacks wisdom, he should ask God who gives generously." If you aren't sure whether a dream is from your child's soul or not, ask God! When we seek Him for wisdom, He will give us the answers we are looking for.

The third source of dreams is Satan or demonic beings. I'm not going to go into great detail about these kinds of dreams, because we already talked about them in an earlier chapter. I will just say, as a rule of thumb, these dreams have a dark setting to them. They usually involve some kind of fear, violence, or perversion. But again, not all of these dreams are going to be dark.

Someone once told me about a dream they had that involved a police officer. The police officer had pulled them over and was interrogating them. The officer starting writing them up and citing them for all these bad things they had done. In the dream, though, they knew they hadn't done *any* of those bad things.

They asked me about the dream because they wanted to know if Jesus was the police officer and He was making them aware of bad things they had done so they could repent. I immediately discerned in my spirit that this police officer was representing a false authority in their life. Satan was trying to make citations against this person through a false authority in their life to make them feel guilt and shame about things they hadn't even done!

In this case, the lighting in the dream wasn't dark, but it had a dark "feeling " to the person. This is a good example of why we can't prescribe formulas to dreams. A formula would say that police officers always equal Jesus and because it wasn't a dark setting it must be from God. We have to look at the big picture and overall feelings to determine the source.

As a parent, you have to trust that still, small voice of God to show you the source of your child's dream. You don't have to figure it out right away. Take time to pray about it to discern the source.

Here's an overview of the general guidelines for determining the source of dreams and imaginations. Just remember there are exceptions to every rule and it will still need prayed about and discerned.

God

- Light setting
- Bright colors
- Fruit of the Spirit present, like peace
- Interaction with Jesus or angels
- Gives us solutions to problems
- Guides us in the right direction
- Keeps us from sin (Genesis 20:6)

Soul

- Muted colors
- Own desires
- Own fears
- Own needs
- Something that has been on our mind a lot
- A feeling or emotion we've been having

Satan

- Dark or nighttime setting
- Fear
- Confusion
- Lies or deceptions
- Unsettledness in our spirits
- Anger or rage
- Dark or cynical characters

Family Activation!

★ As a family, talk about the three sources of dreams and imaginations (or thoughts). Keep talking about it until your children have a basic understanding of how the three are different.

★ Next, talk about different dreams, visions, daydreams, thoughts, etc., that you've each experienced. As a family, decide what the source of each one was. Even if you can't figure them all out, allow each person to have input into the conversation. You don't have to have all the "right" answers. Just talking about it in this way will cause your children to begin to think about what the possible source of their thoughts and dreams might be.

★ If you have already talked to your children about how their imaginations are like a whiteboard, tell them they can now visualize that their whiteboards have three columns — one for each of the three sources. Have them start practicing putting their thoughts into one of the three columns. The rule of thumb is: if it's a thought or dream from God — focus on it. If it's from the soul — learn from it. If it's from Satan — use your authority over it!

Chapter 8
Discovering Dream Language

Another key to understanding your children's dreams is learning their dream language. Our dream language was actually the first language we were given before our native language. We were speaking the language of dreams before we could say, "momma!"

> **Our dream language is as unique as we are. The way we perceive the world around us and the experiences we've had, all determine the language in which we dream.**

Let me give you some examples that will clarify what dream language is and why it's so important to understand. My son is a high thrills kind of guy. He could ride roller coasters all day long and have the time of his life doing it. I'm rather adventurous myself, but my equilibrium has something to say about twisting, turning, and flying around upside down at top speeds. My stomach has something to say about it too!

If my son has a dream he's riding a roller coaster, it would probably mean he's feeling like he's on top of the world and he's enjoying the thrills of life. But if I have a dream about being on one, it would probably indicate that I feel disoriented about life. I'm not enjoying all the twists and turns. I just wish the ups and downs of life would stop so I could get my bearings back!

How could the same dream mean two different things? It's because the interpretation is based on each person's perceptions. This is called dream language. Everyone has their own unique way of viewing the world around them that shapes the language in which they dream.

> **Dream language is why we can't rely on formulas for interpreting dreams. Formulas can be helpful, but it should never become "the way" we interpret dreams. Understanding a person's dream language is far more important than a formula, because it will reveal to you the true meaning of the dream.**

Another classic example is dreaming about a dog. Frequently, a dog represents a best friend in a dream — taken from the old adage that a dog is a man's best friend. Some people love dogs and yet others are terrified of them. If you had a frightful experience as a child with a dog, you might not like them too much as an adult. Everyone's perceptions about dogs is different and based on their own personal likes and dislikes, as well as life experiences.

So if someone who absolutely loves dogs dreams about one, it could represent a best friend in their dream. But if you have a fear of dogs and one is attacking you in your dream, the dog isn't going to represent a friend, but rather a spirit of fear attacking you.

You know your children better than anyone else. You know what their life experiences have been. You have a good idea what their emotions are like, including fears they might have. It's going to be easier for you than anyone else to understand your children's dream languages. Even though your children are all growing up in the same house, each child will have their own way of dreaming based on their perceptions of what life is like.

If you aren't sure what your child's dream language is, ask them! If your child tells you a dream they had about their principal, ask them how they feel about their principal in real life. Once they tell you, it will be a big clue as to what the meaning of the principal was in their dream and what their dream language is.

If they dream about a gorilla, ask them what they know about gorillas. There might be some fact they know about gorillas tucked in their brain that is the key to the meaning of it in their dream. When you ask someone what they think, feel, or know about something in a dream, usually the very first thing that comes out of their mouth is the real meaning. When they have too much time to think about it, then the meaning becomes unclear. It's a classic case of overthinking your answer so always go with their gut responses.

Once you figure out what your child's dream language is, or even your own, you can start to build a "dream dictionary." Write down in a notebook things they consistently dream about and what those things mean to them. This notebook will become a reference point for you to learn their dream language. This will make interpreting their dreams easier in the future.

Here's an example of my dream dictionary. When I dream about my pastor, he usually represents the Holy Spirit . Someone else could dream about my pastor who had an negative experience with him and it would mean something entirely different!

In real life, we have a 5.0 Mustang convertible. When I dream about driving the Mustang, it's usually talking about my personal ministry. I don't like cats, so cats in my dreams are usually evil spirits ... sorry all you cat lovers out there! When I dream about the house I grew up in, it's dealing with a current issue I have that stemmed from my childhood.

Once you start unlocking dream language, then you can start looking at how things are behaving in your dream to give you a better understanding of what the dream is saying. In the case of my Mustang dreams, I look at how I'm interacting with the car for clues to how I'm feeling about where I'm at in life. Since it's a convertible, I had a sense of freedom in the dreams, but sometimes I wasn't really going anywhere. In the dreams, I couldn't get the car in the right gear or it was running out of gas. Sometimes I wanted to go really fast but no matter how hard I pushed on the gas pedal, it just wasn't going anywhere! I felt a lot of frustration in the dream and was equally frustrated about where I was at in real life.

I'm finally just now getting to the point where my car is starting to move in my dreams. I'm waiting for the day, though, when I dream I'm in the Mustang and I'm headed down the road at breakneck speeds! Hummm … maybe God knows best and that's why He doesn't let me press the gas as hard as I'd like!

Mustangs are my dream language. Your children have their own dream language as well. Find out what their language is because this will be a huge key in unlocking the meaning of their dreams. Then, start speaking their language. You can actually pray out things exactly as you see them in dreams and it will be just as effective as if you prayed using "normal" language.

Let's say your child dreams that a mouse got into their room. A cat came along and wanted to catch the mouse, but something was stopping the cat from being able to do that. In this dream, the cat is a good thing (unlike it would be in my dream)! The mouse is an unwanted guest, and a cat was sent to take care of this intruder. However, something is blocking the cat from being able to do its job.

Instead of praying with your child and saying something like, "In Jesus name demon get out of my child's room," (which isn't a bad prayer), you could actually use the language of the dream. You could pray with your child and say something like, "Jesus, I know you sent the cat to get rid of this mouse. Please help the cat to be able to do its job."

This type of prayer would be just as effective and probably a lot less intimidating to a child who might be scared that an intruder was trying to get into their room! Instead, you spoke their dream language and it was in words the child could relate to. Using dream language is safe because you know if the child dreamed it, they have a language or an understanding of it already.

> **Learning your child's dream language will be a powerful key to unlocking the mystery of their dreams!**

Family Activation!

★ Talk to your kids about dream language. As a family, take some common objects and take turns telling what your perceptions or feelings are about those objects. To get you started, here is a list of some common things people dream about. Ask each child what their feelings are about the following:

>Dogs and wolves
>
>House cats and big cats like lions
>
>Flying in an airplane or being on a train
>
>Being in the woods, being at the ocean, etc.
>
>Being at school
>
>Foods and drinks
>
>Being on a bike or in a car
>
>Going to the bathroom (I know this sounds silly but bathroom dreams are incredibly common)

★ If you can, give each of your children a notebook that can become their "Dream Dictionary." Have them start recording common objects they dream about and what those objects represent to them.

Chapter 9
The Language of the Spirit

This year I had the opportunity to go to Peru. While I was there, I did some dream interpretations on the streets. I saw a man sitting on a bench that looked quite "interesting" to say the least, and I felt compelled to go talk to him. This man was traveling the world barefoot and shirtless. He had no home. He was simply traveling from continent to continent, exploring as many religions as possible.

My goal wasn't to get this man saved; I simply wanted to connect him to the Holy Spirit so that when he was ready, he knew how to find Him. I spoke to this man using his "language." Yes, he spoke English, but he also had a language based on his religious beliefs and experiences. I asked the Holy Spirit what language I needed to use in order to talk to this man in a non-threatening, but effective way.

I asked him how he connects with his gods and

he said through meditation. I asked him if he wanted to use meditation to connect with my God. He was very open, and I led him through an encounter with the Holy Spirit, using language which with he was familiar. By the end, the man said that he had encountered a lot of light and a lot of love from the God I showed him.

> **You see, everyone has a language they speak — including the Holy Spirit. Not only do we have our own personal dream language, but there's also a dream language in which the Spirit speaks to us.**

One of the most frustrating parts about being in Peru was the fact that I couldn't speak Spanish. There was a language barrier. When we don't understand the dream language of the Spirit, there is a barrier there as well. I believe when we learn His language, it's another key to unlocking the mystery of dreams.

So what is the language of the Spirit when it comes to dreams? Dreams are all about symbolism. Visions are usually more literal, but dreams are full of symbols. God is using something in the natural that we can relate to or identify with, and He's using it to show us a spiritual parallel. Jesus did this all the time when He was on the earth — it's called parables. Dreams are simply night parables.

If you want to unlock some of the hidden meaning of your children's dreams, it's a really good idea to study the parables in the Bible. Studying the parables will help you start training your mind to think in the language of the Spirit. Here's a quick overview of some of the symbolism Jesus used in parables:

- Parable of the lost sheep (Luke 15:3-7) - the sheep represented sinners.

- Parable of the mustard seed (Luke 13:18) - the seed represented the kingdom of God.

- Parable of the lost coin (Luke 15:8-10) - the coin represented a sinner.

- Parable of the persistent widow (Luke 18:1-8) - showed the disciples they should always pray and never give up.

When you read those parables, ask yourself questions like, "Why does a seed represents the kingdom of God?" or "Why does a sheep represent a sinner?" Reflecting on the parable like this will train your mind to start thinking symbolically.

I always find myself asking questions like, "Why this, God, instead of (fill in the blank)?" If I dream about a bear, I ask God, "Why did you use a bear to speak to me, instead of a mountain lion?" There has to be something that is unique about a bear for God to use that animal in my dream instead of another.

One time I did this with kids at a dream workshop. I listed a bunch of animals on a worksheet. I had the kids list good and bad qualities of each animal. For example, a dog is loyal and trainable but can be biting and defensive. So if you dream a dog was trying to bite you, it could represent a friend who has been loyal to you in the past, but their words have been defensive and "biting" at you lately.

Once you figure out what the good and bad qualities are of a particular animal in your dream, then look at what the animal was doing to determine which quality it was displaying. In this way, you will be able to determine if the animal represents something positive or negative in your dream. Obviously, in the above dream, the dog was representing something negative that was happening in the dreamer's life.

This can be done with more than just animals. Take any object in your dream and start looking at the different qualities or characteristics of it. What makes that object unique and different than anything else?

I say all of this because I want your mind to start processing what certain things might mean, not only in your children's dreams, but your dreams also. Knowing that God speaks in symbols means we have to train our minds to think symbolically so we can understand the language of the Spirit.

Besides reading the parables in the New Testament, study dream interpretations that were given throughout the Bible. These interpretations are examples that will help you better understand the language of God in dreams. There's a website that has a list of every dream recorded in the Bible that I have found to be an excellent resource. I included the name of the website in the footnotes of this book. 8

The very first thing I did when I came home from Peru was start learning Spanish because I knew I was going back again. I wanted to learn the language so I could connect with the people there at a deeper level.

> **When we don't understand the language of how God speaks in dreams, it's like being in a foreign country with no knowledge of the spoken language.**

If we want to connect with God at a deeper level of understanding, it's going to be critical to learn His language. Yes, He speaks *our* language, but it's equally important we understand *His* language, too. If He likes to speak in parables, then study parables. If He likes to speak in symbolism, study symbols.

Even when God spoke directly to His people (not through dreams), He spoke using symbolism. When God was speaking to Abraham in Genesis 22:17, He said, "I will surely bless you and make your descendants as numerous as the stars in the sky and as the sand seashore." God used something in the natural that Abraham could relate to in order to convey a message to him in a way he would understand.

There are examples of God speaking symbolically throughout the entire Bible, and would be a study on its own. The point is, if we want to understand what our dreams and our children's dreams mean, then it's a good idea to have some understanding of how God speaks. Reading His word is a good way to learn the language that He likes to speak. Learning the language of the Spirit will help you unlock more of the mysteries of dreams.

Family Activation!

★ As a family, read some of the parables found in the New Testament. I always think it's fun to act out the Bible, so if you can, allow your kids to act out the parables as you read them out loud. Here's a list of some good ones that can be easily acted out.

- The wise and foolish builders — Matthew 7:24-27
- The sower — Mark 4:3-8
- The good Samaritan — Luke 10:30-37
- The good Shepherd — John 10:1-16
- The prodigal son — Luke 15:11-32
- Laborers in the vineyard — Matthew 20:1-16
- The Great Banquet — Matthew 22:2-9
- The pearl of great value — Matthew 13:45-46

★ After you have acted out the parables, talk about what the different elements represented. Tell your kids that Jesus is still speaking in parables today through dreams! Encourage them to start seeing their dreams as a parable. You could even make a book of family parables that you receive through dreams.

Chapter 10
Creating a Culture of Dreaming

Once you start unlocking the mystery of your children's dreams, it's going to be important to create a culture of dreaming in your home. I want to start off by defining the word "culture." This is the definition of culture according to Merriam-Webster: 1. The beliefs, customs, arts, etc., of a particular society, group, or place. 2. A particular society that has its own beliefs, ways of life, art, etc. 3. A way of thinking, behaving, or working that exists in a place.

Creating a culture of dreaming in your home is taking your beliefs about dreams and creating an atmosphere for dreaming to come alive. I love that the definition of culture includes the arts, because creating this type of atmosphere is an opportunity for creativity to overflow in your home. So, how do you create a culture of dreaming?

First, talk about dreams! Make dreams a part of

your daily conversations. Breakfast is a great time to talk about dreams! If your family isn't able to eat breakfast together, make it your routine to talk about them at the dinner table or before bed. Making dreams a part of your daily conversation will create an atmosphere of expectancy for more dreams.

Talking about dreams with your kids doesn't mean you have to have all the answers. Even if you do have an idea what their dreams mean, I would recommend not telling your children right away. I've been talking to my daughter about dreams ever since she could talk. When she started telling me her dreams, I would tell *her* to ask the Holy Spirit for the interpretation, instead of giving her my interpretation right away. She would then go off and play. A little while later she would come back and tell me that while she was playing, God told her what the dream meant. The funny thing is, the interpretation that she received was always way better than what I had come up with!

In this way, as early as five years old she was able to receive the interpretation to her dreams. Sometimes it's best not to give our kids all the answers. Teach them to hear directly from the Holy Spirit because they will receive greater revelation that way. That doesn't mean you can't discuss with them your thoughts about the dream. I would, however, suggest you have them ask the Holy Spirit first so they don't begin to rely on you for the interpretation.

Another way you can create a culture of dreaming in your home is to have your kids respond to their dreams. One time my daughter had a very significant dream. She took time to pray about it, and then she received an interpretation. I told her to ask the Holy Spirit what He wanted her to do with the interpretation. She felt the Holy Spirit told her to write a letter and warn people about what she saw in her dream. I helped her write the letter, and then we prayed about who should receive it. We came up with some names and mailed out the letters. I was validating to my daughter that her dreams were important. Even if she didn't have the interpretation exactly right, I was teaching her to respond to the messages that God was giving her.

Having your kids respond to their dreams will open up the door for them to have more dreams. Luke 16:10 says, "If you are faithful in the little things, you will be faithful in the large ones." When your kids make a response to even a small dream, they are sending God a message that they value their dreams. The more they value their dreams, the more dreams they will have and the greater the messages in the dreams. When we don't respond to dreams, we're also sending God a message. This time the message is that we don't value dreams enough to allow them to shape our lives.

So, what would a response to a dream look like? This can take on many forms. I can't give you a definitive list of responses, but I can give you some examples. One time I had a dream that I was buying oranges from a man in my church. He was selling them for a low price, and I thought they were worth more. I gave him $5 in the dream for the oranges. There was a message in the dream about how this man saw his worth. I told the man the interpretation, then I gave him a $5 bill as a physical representation of the spiritual application of the dream.

Another time I had a dream about a well-known prophetic leader. In the dream, he was helping some of my friends become free from their bondages. I gave him $20 in the dream for helping my friends. When I woke up, I knew I needed to send this man $20 as a physical representation of the dream. I was hoping this man wouldn't be offended by such a small donation to his ministry, however, it really wasn't about the *amount* of money. It was about making a response in the natural that I felt would release a spiritual reaction.

A response isn't always going to require a physical object. Often, a response can be a change in behavior. If God shows you in a dream something you are doing that you shouldn't be, then stop doing it! Or, if

Creating a Culture of Dreaming

He shows you something that you *should* be doing, then do it! The best response to a dream is simply to ask the Holy Spirit what He wants you to do with the dream. Asking the Spirit for guidance is a response in itself!

In addition to talking about dreams and asking the Holy Spirit if we need to respond to them, we can also create a culture of dreaming by encouraging our kids to record their dreams. Remember the definition of culture included the arts? This is where you can get creative! Probably one of the most boring way for kids to write down their dreams is line by line. You don't want recording dreams to become just another tedious homework assignment. You want them to be excited about doing it! It should be an opportunity for an overflow of creativity.

Anytime kids can engage the right side of their brains (where creative thoughts come from), it actually helps them to remember more of the details of the dream. As they are being creative, parts of the dream will emerge that they had forgotten about. Here's a list of some creative ways kids can record their dreams:

- Paint a scene
- Use modeling clay to shape something they saw
- Act it out like Charades
- Write it on white paper with a white crayon and then put watercolors on top of the writing

- Draw pictures
- Write it out in the format of a comic strip
- Draw a rainbow and in each arc write one sentence about something that happened
- If they like soccer, draw soccer balls and write one sentence about the dream inside each ball
- Pretend they are a news reporter and their dream is the top story, then videotape them telling it

The point is, make it fun! Let your kids make journaling their dreams an exciting time of the day. It's not necessary that they write down every detail of the dream. I tell kids to pretend they are reporters when recording their dreams. Reporters just tell the main facts. Daniel 7:1 says, "Daniel had a dream and visions of his head while on his bed. Then he wrote down the dream, telling the main facts." If they can remove a detail from the dream and it doesn't change the overall meaning, then it's not a detail they have to write down.

By doing the things we talked about, you will be creating an environment where dreams can be celebrated. God loves a good celebration in His honor! Celebrating dreams in your home by talking about them, writing them down, and responding to them, is like inviting God to the party. When He shows up, He'll release even more dreams in your home. And that is how a culture of dreaming is created in your home!

Family Activation!

★ Time to get creative as a family! Choose one dream that someone in your house had recently. I would recommend picking a short, easy dream. Each person in your family will record the same dream but in different ways. Perhaps one of you could act it out, one could paint it, one could make a news story about it, and one could turn it into a comic strip.

★ After you are done, discuss as many creative ideas as you can think of for recording dreams in the future. Then, start putting it into practice!

★ Next, make a commitment to create a culture of dreaming in your home. Take time to talk about your kids' dreams each day. Encourage your kids to ask the Holy Spirit how they should respond to their dreams. Take time to celebrate dreams as a family. You could even put together a family slumber party to celebrate dreams with popcorn and hot chocolate!

Chapter 11

Mystery Solved...or is it?

I love a good mystery. I think that's why God intrigues me so much, because He's so mysterious. I enjoy the fact that as soon as I figure out one mystery, there's another one waiting to be solved.

I like to think I've solved a few of the mysteries of dreams, but the fact is there's a billion more things about dreams that I haven't unlocked yet. And, that excites me! I know it can be really frustrating when you want to know what a dream means and you can't solve that mystery, but sometimes the act of seeking out the answer is more important than the answer itself!

Countless times I have had dreams that made me wonder what kind of trippy pizza I ate before bed, yet I know in my spirit it had a profound meaning. So I would spend the entire day just asking the Holy Spirit questions like, "Well, what about this? Yeah, but why that?" I'm pretty sure He hides the meaning from me sometimes just so we can spend the day together talking about it!

Dreams are the same way for your children. God is connecting with your children Spirit to spirit through dreams. He's drawing them into a one-on-one conversation with Him. The bigger picture of dreams is all about relationship. God is building a relationship with your children through dreams and encounters in the night that draw them closer to Him.

So do you want to know what the real key is to unlocking your children's dreams? Being okay with leaving parts of the mystery UNsolved! Trust that the process of solving the mystery is more important than the mystery itself, because the mystery is what draws us into the relationship.

This is only going to work, though, if we are actually drawing near. If we have a belief system that dreams don't really mean anything, then we're going to miss the invitation into the relationship. Be at peace with not knowing all the answers, but don't let that be an excuse for not asking the questions. Encourage your children to ask as many questions as they want, then wait for answers that the Holy Spirit wants to reveal.

Job 33:15-16 says, "In a dream, in a vision of the

night, when deep sleep falls upon men, while slumbering on their beds, then He opens the ears of men, and seals their instruction." How you ever wondered about that last part—"seals their instruction?"

One time I had a dream that my mom (who is in heaven) came to me. I knew there was this great barrier between us that I wasn't allowed to pass. My mom started teaching me all about ranks, names, and purposes of angels. I woke up from that dream and I could remember every detail *except* for one ... the actual teaching itself!!

Then I had a dream and I was taught all about the rank, names, and purposes of demons. I woke up and remembered everything about the dream *except* for one thing ... yep, the actual teaching itself!

This is a picture of what Job was talking about when he said, "and seals their instruction." Those teachings have been sealed in my spirit. I don't have access to them right now. But I have confidence that when I need to know those things, the seal will be broken and the mystery revealed. I'm resolved with the mystery being sealed for now because it keeps me hungry for more. I think God reveals just enough of the mystery to keep me coming back for more.

Even though there might be parts of your dreams

that you have to leave unsolved, there will be plenty that God *will* reveal. Daniel 2:24 says, "Surely your God is the God of gods and the Lord of kings and a revealer of mysteries." When I have a perplexing dream, I "remind" God that He is the revealer of mysteries. I thank Him that He delights in revealing things to me that are impossible for me to know on my own.

If you read the very next verse after Job 33:15-16, it tells us why the full mystery of dreams isn't always revealed — "to keep them from pride." If we knew the entirety of the mystery, I wonder how much pride we might have? I wonder if we would stop relying on the Holy Spirit so much?

I say all this because I don't want you to feel discouraged if you are having trouble understanding your children's dreams. It's a process, and we have to come to terms with how the process works. Some things will be revealed, and other things will remain hidden. Despite the name of this book, "Unlocking the Mystery of Children's Dreams," you'll never be able to fully unlock all the mysteries of your children's dreams. That's the fun part!

Start a journey with your kids. Ask the Holy Spirit to begin to reveal keys to them that will unlock certain aspects of their dreams. There are so many doors to discovering how God speaks in dreams, that they can spend an entire lifetime gaining new keys.

Have you ever seen how many keys a custodian carries around? I remember once asking a high school custodian for a key. He pulled out a key ring the size of a dinner plate, browsed through enough keys to unlock an entire city block, and went directly to the one I needed. I often wondered if that guy ever got tired of carrying around an extra ten pounds of keys with him.

When you ask God for keys to unlocking your dreams, you are becoming a spiritual custodian. God likes to give us keys that unlock certain aspects of dreams. The more we can be trusted, the more keys He gives us. Before you know it, you're carrying around more keys to dreams than a high school custodian!

All those keys do come with a certain amount of weight to them. What are we doing with all that extra weight? Are we using those keys to help others gain access into different aspects of dreaming? Are we sharing those keys with our children?

I've been studying, meditating, and seeking God about dreams for the past 15 years, and yet I feel like I know so little about them. I do know that I've gained *some* keys, though, because I've been willing to spend time searching for them. Matthew 7:7 says, "Ask and it will be given to you; seek and you will find; knock and the door will be opened to you." When we ask God for more keys to understanding dreams, He responds and gives us more. When we are seeking answers, He will show us where to find them. And when we knock on His door and ask for more, He will open the door to us.

When a friend comes to your door and knocks, you open the door to them and invite them inside. Every time we ask for keys and we're seeking understanding, it's another knock on God's door. He's comes to the door and He invites to us to come in to more and more understanding.

The purpose of this book was to share with you some of the keys that I've spent time searching for and knocking on God's door to receive. I want to be able to open some of the doors for you and your children to understand the realm of dreaming in less time than it took me. We might not have unlocked all the mysteries to your children's dreams in this book, but I do hope we jiggled a few locks loose!

Family Activation!

★ It's time for your journey to begin to discovering keys to dreaming! Before you start this activation, hide keys around your house. It can be old keys that you don't need anymore or you can order really cheap keys online. Hide them in places that your kids really have to search to find them.

★ Start off by reviewing some of the main ideas from this chapter. Tell your kids that as a family you are going to ask God to reveal keys to you about dreams and their meanings. Tell them that you have hidden keys around the house that you want them to go find.

★ Once your kids have found the keys and come back, explain to them that God has keys for them to find as well. His keys will help them better understand how He speaks through dreams. It might not be a physical key but they are gaining spiritual ones. The physical keys that they found will be reminders of the spiritual ones they are searching for.

★ Anytime you feel like someone in your family has received a key to understanding dreams, write it down in your family journal or dream book.

End Notes

a. Lifenews.com article titled "Unborn Babies Can Dream in the Womb, Will Abortions be Their Nightmares?"

b. Webmd.com

c. Bettersleep.org articled titled "REM Sleep"

d. Mentalfloss.com

e. Clevelandclinic.org articled titled "Nightmares"

f. Sleepforkids.org article titled "Children's Sleep Problems: What They Are an How to Deal With Them"

g. http://overviewbible.com/wp-content/uploads/2014/02/infographic.bibledreams.png